Thunder And Lightning ......

saiqah salim

BookLeaf Publishing

Presentation by *BookLeaf Publishing*

Web: www.bookleafpub.com

E-mail: info@bookleafpub.com

ISBN:978-93-95223-09-6

First edition 2022

DEDICATION

This collection is dedicated to me, myself and I
as in moments of insanity I kept myself alive
......

ACKNOWLEDGEMENT

Thank you for being part of the journey and not the destination.

Darkness

In the depth of my own darkness
The broken pieces of my heart
Were entangled in your drowning screams
Your selfless love wanted to rescue me
I wanted to be tangled
In your drowning screams forever …..

Blood And Thunder

Every chapter was filled with blood
Thunder searching for sunsets and rainbows
She was forever drowning in storms
Still rising to chase her beautiful dreams
Covered in rainbow blood …….

Letting Go

The art of letting go is a painful process
Slowly slowly it tears your heart
Rips your soul apart
It takes you to the depth of your own darkness
Then you realise your self-worth
The art of letting go
Creates a beautiful journey
Of self-discovery, self-love
A stronger you is created...........

Red Mist

Loving you was red
On the brink of insanity
The red mist between
Sane and insane
Even in those moments
Loving you was red
The life in my soul
The roses in my veins …….

I Bleed Roses

I bleed roses from the core of my soul
Drowning every wish, hope and prayer
In the fragrance of my heart's desires
I bleed roses running through my veins
Sketching your everlasting promises
On my soul word by word
Entangled in moments
Justifying your existence
Forever I bleed roses ………..

Rainbows And Oceans

After the darkest thunderstorm
Upon the rising sun
Her soul blooms
Magic and madness
Over the rainbows
Under the oceans ....

Healing

Tear upon tear
I've created oceans
In my destiny
It is written healing
Should create something beautiful ....

Sanity

Searching for you
Over the rainbows
Under the oceans
Loving the journey
Of magic and madness
Always testing my sanity
The hope to survive
Capture everlasting moments
With you ……...

Rainbow Teardrops

Searching for answers
In the ocean of tears
Drowning in rainbow teardrops
Filled with the colours of our love
My dreams
Your promises
The harsh reality
Of betrayal …….

Kiss Me Like Poetry

Kiss me like poetry
Running hope through my veins
Embracing the magic in my heart
Kiss me like poetry
Raging raw emotions
Capturing my soul
Giving me strength to soldier on
Re-living a fairy tale
Forever lost in heartbeats
And thunderstorms ………

Chasing Rainbows

Living in denial
Trying to escape reality
Delusional or insane
Trying to erase
Those things that are true
Those feelings felt
Chasing the rainbows
Drowning in the storms
Seeking perfection
Losing my sanity
Closing chapters
Dying in hope
Relighting my
Sheer existence
To rise again ……..

Searching

Backlash to betrayal
Still Searching for my soul's peace
Forever testing destiny
Whilst hanging onto a caged heart
Surviving on a thread of hope ……

Flowers Bloom

Life is a land of pain
Still flowers bloom
Where wounded soldiers die
Life is a land of pain
Still flowers bloom
In the resting place of loved ones
Life is a land of pain
Still flowers bloom
On the paths where lovers parted
Life is a land of pain
Still flowers bloom
In the hearts of those who live in hope ……...

Reality

Forgotten footsteps
Broken dreams
Erasing the memories
Of all those whispered lies
Raging in my mind
Always in denial
Never giving up hope
Gentle was your touch
Everlasting was my promise
Reality was the betrayal ……

My Sanity

Invading space
In My withering soul
Seeking solace
In my own space
My eyes forever
Seeking that place
Wishing for a few
Peaceful moments
I don't see you
I don't hear you
I am just me
In my minds
Own thoughts and space ……...

Hope

As the night is creeping in
Whisper me some magic
Captured in breath-taking moments
Paint my nightmares
In the colours of hope
Wrapped in madness
On the brink of insanity ……

Moments

This heart of mine
Is still in love
With those moments
Your lips touched my forehead ……

Silent Prayers

The poem I never posted
As I've not yet healed from that chapter
The silent prayers still whispered
The hope of destiny changing, still lingers
The deep feelings filled with raw emotions
Leaving my eyes drowning and my soul
crumbling ……...

Ammunition

Emotions shouldn't be shared with everyone
Every word you say
One day will be used as ammunition
Fired back at you
Believe me
That shit cuts deep …...

Home

The serenity of the prayer mat
The silence of the night
It's not much but it's home
The whispers of dreams
The tears of heartache
It's not much but it's home
The moments and memories
The madness and magic
It's not much but it's home ….

Salute

Middle finger salute
To all the fantasies
That never made it
Past the first page …...